Catherine Zeta Jones

Sandra Woodcock

Published in association with The Basic Skills Agency

Hodder & Stoughton
A MEMBER OF THE HODDER HEADLINE GROUP

Acknowledgements
Cover: © All Action
Photos: p. 2 © HTV; p. 5 © The Ronald Grant Archive; pp. 9, 11, 26 © The Kobal Collection; p. 13 © PA Photos; p. 20 © Alpha; p. 24 © AP Photo/Leslie Hassler.

Every effort has been made to trace copyright holders of material reproduced in this book. Any rights not acknowledged will be acknowledged in subsequent printings if notice is given to the publisher.

Orders: please contact Bookpoint Ltd, 130 Milton Park, Abingdon, Oxon OX14 4SB. Telephone: (44) 01235 827720, Fax: (44) 01235 400454. Lines are open from 9.00 – 6.00, Monday to Saturday, with a 24 hour message answering service. Email address: orders@bookpoint.co.uk

British Library Cataloguing in Publication Data
A catalogue record for this title is available from The British Library

ISBN 0 340 84883 9

First published 2002
Impression number   10 9 8 7 6 5 4 3 2 1
Year   2007 2006 2005 2004 2003 2002

Copyright © 2002 Sandra Woodcock

All rights reserved. No part of this publication may be reproduced or transmitted in any form or by any means, electronic or mechanical, including photocopying, recording, or any information storage and retrieval system, without permission in writing from the publisher or under licence from the Copyright Licensing Agency Limited. Further details of such licences (for reprographic reproduction) may be obtained from the Copyright Licensing Agency Limited, of 90 Tottenham Court Road, London W1P 9HE.

Typeset by SX Composing DTP, Rayleigh, Essex.
Printed in Great Britain for Hodder & Stoughton Educational, a division of Hodder Headline Plc, 338 Euston Road, London NW1 3BH by The Bath Press Ltd.

Contents

		Page
1	The Girl from Wales	1
2	The Price of Fame	6
3	Hollywood	8
4	Just a Pretty Face?	12
5	The Man in her Life	13
6	The Wedding	17
7	Links with Wales	21
8	The Future	25

1 The Girl from Wales

Catherine was born on 25 September 1969.
She was born in Swansea, Wales.
Her father, Dai, owned a sweet shop.
Her father was Welsh and
her mother, Pat, was Irish.
Catherine has two brothers.
They are a strong family.
Even today, they work together
and give Catherine support.

Catherine Jones is a common name in Wales,
but you don't often hear the name Zeta.
Catherine was named Zeta
after her grandmother.
The name Catherine comes from
her other grandmother, Catherine Fair.

Catherine (right) dressed for her part in the stage production of *Annie*.

Catherine started singing and dancing
at the age of four.
She was 15 when she got a big break.
It was a part in a musical.
She would have to tour for nine months.
It would mean missing her exams.
But Catherine knew
that she wanted to be in show business.
She did not want to miss this chance.
Her mum and dad backed her.
So Catherine left Wales
and began her career in Liverpool.

In 1984 she moved to London.
She was in another musical
called *42nd Street*.
Catherine was lucky.
She got the chance to play the lead
because the star of the show hurt her leg.
Catherine was asked to take over and
she played the part for three years.

Catherine worked really hard.
She was doing eight shows a week.
When she wasn't in the show,
she had jazz dance classes
and ballet classes.
She had to do voice exercises
and practise her singing.
She had no time to herself,
but she was doing something that
she had always wanted to do.

In 1990, she went to Paris.
She had a part in her first film.
Catherine liked film work
and wanted to do more.
In 1991, she was back in Britain.
She had a part in a TV series
called *The Darling Buds of May*.
It was this series
that made her famous in Britain.
Suddenly everyone knew who she was.

Catherine in *The Darling Buds of May* in 1992.

2 The Price of Fame

It was good to be so successful.
But fame has a price.
The press hounded Catherine
and she lost her privacy.
The press saw her as a sex symbol.
Catherine found this hard
but she had to learn how to live with it.
There were cameras outside her London home
most of the time.
Her life had changed for ever.

In the next few years
Catherine had parts in other films
and TV series.
She dated the singer Mick Hucknall,
and John Leslie, who presented
the children's TV show *Blue Peter*.

The press took a great interest
in her love life.
They printed a photo of her
kissing the actor Paul McGann.
They were co-stars in a film at the time.
But Paul was just a friend.
It was a friendly kiss.
Paul was married
and the press made out that Catherine
was someone who steals husbands.
Catherine had had enough.
Her career was going nowhere
and her private life was public news.

Soon after this she went to the USA
for a new film called *The Phantom*.
She had a visa for one year.
It was a chance for a fresh start.
She would stay in the USA.
Was she running away
or moving on?

3 Hollywood

Catherine was hoping that her career
would take off in the USA.
She went to lots of parties.
She wanted to make useful contacts.
She took a part in a TV series
called *Titanic*.
It wasn't very good,
but it got her face on TV.

Then she had a lucky break.
She was seen by Steven Spielberg.
He liked the look of Catherine.
He gave her the chance to star
in a new Hollywood film.
It was called *The Mask of Zorro*.
It was an adventure film
with a touch of humour.
They filmed in Mexico.
Catherine's co-stars were
Antonio Banderas and Anthony Hopkins.

Catherine in *The Mask of Zorro*.

Catherine worked hard on this film.
It is a film with lots of action,
and Catherine showed off her dancing skills.
But there were new skills to learn:
sword-fencing and horse-riding.
She was good at sword-fencing,
but she had to take a few falls
before she could ride a horse.
The hard work paid off, though.
The film was a smash hit.

The Mask of Zorro made Catherine famous
and it led to more offers of work.
She had many new fans.
One of them was Sean Connery.
He wanted her to star with him
in a new film, called *Entrapment*.
In the film the two of them play
a pair of jewel thieves.
Connery is much older than Catherine.
He was 68 and she was only 29
when the film was made.
Some people said the love affair in the plot
was hard to believe,
because of their age difference.
But Catherine has always liked older men.

Catherine with Sean Connery in *Entrapment*.

4 Just a Pretty Face?

When Catherine was born,
her parents said she looked like a frog!
Now she has been voted
one of the world's most beautiful women.
She has long dark hair and brown eyes.
Her good looks have won her many fans
and must have played a part in her success.
She says: 'I think beauty is a gift
that you have to make the most of.
I've worked very hard to try to look my best.'

But in Hollywood there are plenty
of good-looking women.
You need talent to be a success.
When she was young, Catherine spent years
learning to act, to sing and to dance.
She has had some lucky breaks,
but she works hard on her skills
as well as on her looks.

5   The Man in her Life

Catherine wanted more than a good career.
She wanted a husband and children.
Then she met a man she liked very much.
His name was Michael Douglas.
He was a famous actor and film producer.
He was handsome and rich,
with a fortune of £150 million.
His father, Kirk Douglas,
was one of Hollywood's biggest stars.

Michael first saw Catherine
in *The Mask of Zorro*.
He met her in 1998
at a film festival in France,
and he fell in love with her.
Michael was 54.
He had been married before
and he had a grown-up son.

Catherine fell in love with Michael Douglas, the Hollywood actor and film producer.

Catherine and Michael spent
a lot of time together.
It was no surprise
when he bought her a ring.
It was a £2 million
diamond engagement ring.
Michael asked Catherine
to marry him.

Soon Catherine was pregnant.
Their baby was born in August 2000.
Catherine and Michael had a son.
The baby was named Dylan.
A very Welsh name!

They began to plan their wedding.
The press took a great interest
in the plans.

Michael wanted Catherine to sign
a contract before the wedding.
This would limit how much money
she could take from him
if the marriage ended.
He had already paid his first wife
£44 million when they divorced.
Catherine wanted something
in the contract to say
she would be paid £3 million
if Michael cheated on her.

This all seems a long way
from love and romance!
But it is common
in Hollywood marriages.

6 The Wedding

There were many questions
about the wedding.
Where would it be?
Would it be a quiet wedding
in a small church in Wales?
Or would it be a big
Hollywood wedding
5000 kilometres away?
When would it be?
Catherine and Michael share
the same birthday: 25 September.
Would the wedding be
on their joint birthday in 2000?
How many famous people
would be invited?

At last the date was fixed.
They would be married
on Saturday 18 November.
The wedding would take place
in the Plaza Hotel, New York.
There was so much interest from the press
that Catherine and Michael
made a deal with one magazine.
OK! paid £1 million for the rights
to photos of the wedding.

When the big day came,
Catherine's family were there to see it.
She had a private jet to fly them
from Wales to New York.
Even Zeta, her 85 year-old gran, was there.
There were 350 guests at the wedding.
Many of them were famous names
and big stars.
Tom Hanks, Steven Spielberg and
Anthony Hopkins, to name just a few.

Catherine's wedding ring came from Wales.
It was made of Welsh gold.
She was a beautiful bride.
Her dress was made of ivory satin.
And the train was lace.
Michael's best man was
his 21 year-old son, Cameron.
Baby Dylan was also there.
Catherine's mum, Pat, held him
and he was very well-behaved!

The wedding cake was
well over a metre high
and had five tiers.
The cake alone cost £7000.
The total cost of the wedding
was well over £1 million.

7 Links with Wales

Catherine now has the life
of a Hollywood superstar.
But she will not forget
her Welsh background.
The people of her home town
are proud of Catherine.

A new Welsh link
to the name Zeta has been found.
In the 1860s, Henry Bath of Swansea
had a ship called the *Zeta*.
It was well-known for carrying copper
from South America to Swansea.
Catherine's middle name
may come from this bit of Welsh history!

Catherine is one of Hollywood's biggest stars, but she never forgets her roots.

In Wales it is an old custom
to send a lovespoon to a bride and groom.
These are wooden spoons
with carving on them.
They are good-luck tokens.

The people of Swansea
sent Catherine and Michael
a Welsh lovespoon.
On it was a heart for love,
a bell for the wedding,
and a two-link chain to show
two lives joined together.

Catherine and Michael gave
a silver Welsh lovespoon
to each of the guests at the wedding.

The people of Swansea
have sent story books
in the Welsh language for baby Dylan.
Catherine and her new family visit Wales
to see old friends and family.

There are rumours that
one of her next films
will be about a Welsh rugby team.
She will produce and star in it.

If Catherine ever gets tired
of her Hollywood life,
she will always find
a warm welcome in Wales.

Catherine with her co-stars of *America's Sweethearts*.

8 The Future

Catherine seems to be a woman
who has everything.
Her life is good at the moment.
But what lies in the future?
Catherine would like
to have more children
and she will make more films.
She and her brother
have a film company
called Milkwood Films.
Even the name of this company has
a link with Wales –
Under Milk Wood was a poem
by the Welsh poet, Dylan Thomas.

She starred with Julia Roberts in the
film, *America's Sweethearts*, in 2001.
In the movie she plays a beautiful
Hollywood actress, and Julia Roberts
plays her frumpy sister!

Catherine in the 2001 film, *Traffic*.

Also in 2001, she starred with
Michael Douglas in the film *Traffic*.
It is about drug wars in America.
Perhaps they will make more films together.
There may be a new Zorro film.

Going to America
was a good move for Catherine.
In January 2002, she was named
the highest-paid British woman in Hollywood.
With her success and her contacts,
She seems well placed to achieve
whatever she wants in life.